Advance praise for *One Steady Glance*:

"One of the greatest joys of life is spending time with art which invites you to spend time with your emotions by reflecting on someone else's experiences. Jeff Price's book of poetry is such a dalliance. From cars to Camelot, high school wrestling and the highest of lifeforms—the dog, Price's *One Steady Glance* uses content and craft to allow readers to indulge in beautiful poetry while learning more about their own journey."

—Russell Minatel, colleague and friend

"One might be forgiven for calling Jeff Price a warrior poet--while complimentary, it doesn't do justice to the full weight *One Steady Glance* evokes in the reader's spirit. Price's verse is an immersion in all the sins and grace, pettiness and nobility, strength and weakness, anger and love, the sadness and gratitude, and the struggles and joys of a life, not perfect or great, but rather lived greatly in its imperfections--and through those perfect imperfections, the reader might just find the forgiveness, hope, and inspiration to find the warrior and poet within themselves."

—Will Koella, friend and former student

ONE STEADY GLANCE

COLLECTED POEMS

JEFF PRICE

REDHAWK
PUBLICATIONS

Copyright © 2023 Jeff Price

All rights reserved. This book or parts thereof may not be reproduced in any form, stored in any retrieval system, or transmitted in any form by any means—electronic, mechanical, photocopy, recording, or otherwise—without prior written permission of the publisher, except as provided by United States of America copyright law. For permission requests, write to the publisher, at "Attention: Permissions Coordinator," at the address below.

Redhawk Publications
The Catawba Valley Community College Press
2550 US Hwy 70 SE
Hickory NC 28602

ISBN: 978-1-959346-02-9

Library of Congress Number: 2022952035

Printed in the United States of America

redhawkpublications.com

"I am trying to hold in one steady glance all the parts of my life."

—Adrienne Rich, *Toward the Solstice*

To Julie
Who stands between me and outer darkness

To Kade
Who got me off my ass and back in the game

To Tyler and Kaylen
Whose art motivates me to make my own

TABLE OF CONTENTS

Glances at Family
Falcon Dreaming   15
Their Proper End   17
Tyler   19
Lights on the Half-Life   20
In Case Anyone Wonders   21
Warmth   22
Crane   23
Only Now   24
Seventeen   26
Sweet Hat   28

Glances at Classrooms
Fire, Miracle, and Love   33
Trying to Teach Rich with Twenty-Three Days of School   34
Catching Muses in an Empty Room   37
Fourteen   38
Look   41
You Can't Write a Poem About Virtual Graduates   43
Pats on the Fire Line   45
Thirty-Two   46

Glances at Elegies
Gifts   51
Scars   52
Two Years Gone   54
Hands   55
Where Were the Bells?   57

Glances Outside
Sanctuary   61
Dreary Intercourse   63
Ode to the Smokies   66
Little Bighorn   68
Beartooth Pass   69

Andrews Bald	70
In Praise of Rain	72
Milligan Station on The Tweetsie Trail	73

Glances at Forms

The Sleep	77
Prine	78
The Table	79
The Grail	80
Three Crowns, Three Hundred, Three Thousand	81
de la Rocha's Keys	82

Glances at Random

Jesus of Mitchell	87
The Heaven of Hillbillies	88
Rhode Island Plate	90
Hymn to Halloween	91

Glances Inside

Pendragon and Perez	97
Song of Myself #13	98
Not for the Lovers	99
Time Stand Still	100
Emrys	101
No Matter	102
Chainsong	104
Musing	105
To Prufrock	106
Hidden, Found	108
Lessons from a Storm	109
What I can and Can't	111

FOREWORD

He arrived just before the sun.

That's how I remember that first meeting. Six o'clock in the morning and still dark, emerging from his truck with Soundgarden's "Spoon Man" blaring at full blast from his speakers, his leg slightly lifted as he played air guitar on it. This seemed to be his only dance move. I thought he was a student, some fifth year senior who had failed on purpose to anchor one more year on the football team's offensive line. This was all but confirmed with the way the other students talked to him; laughing, joking, wrestling. But he wasn't a student, he was some other worldly amalgamation of a teacher and a coach, built like a Sherman tank and existing to mold our minds and bodies into something worth a damn. In many ways he was the harbinger of our doom. Some final boss we had to contend with before entering adulthood.

I was just a shy and awkward 85 pound Freshman who was told if I wanted to make the soccer team I needed to show up at the school 2 hours before class to meet the coach and run 5 miles, 3 times a week. So run I did, having my mother or father shuttle me on their way to work, not realizing what an inconvenience it was at the time. In my own world as every 15 year old is. I had no idea at that time that he had ulterior motives in mind for me, recruiting me onto his wrestling team (his real athletic pursuit and interest, soccer being a casual paycheck), drafting me into his English class, instilling in me a work ethic I've carried with me in all my worldly pursuits.

Throughout my life he's been a mentor and friend, taking a personal interest in my happiness and success, putting up with me through my sarcastic and unbearable years, encouraging me through my many failures, burying my father and performing my wedding ceremony. Even when I've quit on him at times, a cardinal sin in his book, he's always given me the benefit of the doubt, never casting me aside. A true teacher in every sense. For his part I've seen him grow and change in a myriad of ways. Ways most "intelligent" people refuse to. He has honestly weighed the arguments of life throughout his years. I've seen him soften his stance on many topics and take up arms in battles I never expected him to. It says a lot about a man when you can break his life down into real chapters of growth. I tried to capture this in a poem I wrote about him, seeing all of the lives he has touched and shaped in such varying ways over the years. Knowing I was only a small part of it, but never insignificant to him. The only way I could think of to describe this ability was to write the line, "I cannot say I knew him, only that I knew him when." I stand by that assessment.

Speaking of writing, he is also responsible for introducing me to this loneliest of pursuits known as poetry. For that I suppose he has a lot to answer for. It is both a rewarding and maddening act, full of sadness in search of beauty. Killing yourself to stay alive. I felt a tinge of shame when I got published before him, like the universe was doing something ass backwards. I remember telling him "This is all thanks to you. If I'm getting published, it's like you are as well." It's gratifying to see him finally collecting a volume of his work together not only for every student he's ever taught to carry with them, but to pass down to their children as well. The teacher need not stop teaching just because the bell has rung. Class will, forever, go on.

Kincaid Jenkins
Author of *Drinking With Others*

Glances at Family

Falcon Dreaming

for Red Price

Somewhere,
In some resting place for wrecks,
I am fairly sure it now lies lifeless
Rotten rubber overborne by weeds,
Cracking vinyl succumbed to decay,
That old Ford 200 forever silenced
A desk in a salvage yard schoolhouse,
Where, in another sadly too late time,
I learn from the ghost of my father.

Hazy like the thick summer heat
That lies captive in places like this,
Stark like the brisk autumn wind
Trapped colder in these broken shells,
The lesson comes to me just now
How crawling through husks of cars
In my now near spectral childhood,
Teaches me today to see two poems,
One crafted by a more adept other,
One from my own halting brain,
And I remember that one simple miracle
Wrought by the wrench of my dad
Twenty-five dollars worth of lifeless tin
That allegedly "wouldn't never run",
Resurrected by his hard, greasy hands,
To be party to driving lessons and dates,
Six more years of one thing and another
Only again losing its second happy life
When its savior loosed the grip on his.

So often I release the wheel of my youth,
But today I see clearly the words on paper
And I see the sweet, rusty old contraption,
And through tears of sporadic remembrance
Look on the hazy, stoic, lovely face of my father
Tinkering on in the junkyard of the dead,
Looking for life where there should be none,
And finding it, and giving it to us both.

Their Proper End

for Evelyn Price

So often,

Random events have come,
Not birthdays, or milestones,
Or moments long waited for,
But odd things, on odd days,
At odd times, so many ounces
Against the weight of a life,
Which, on looking deeper
Have commanded some act of memory
Or carried some lesson:
Daddy and his junked cars,
Baseball over the radio,
Collisions with brothers-in-law,
Days and times forever kept,
That happened for something,
To teach me some strong truth,
Evermore enlightening,
Forever purposeful,
But sometimes too late.

Like last Tuesday,
Eight miles below Abingdon,
Riding like I stole something,
Partly because I could,
Partly to beat the rain,
But mostly to get back to you,
To see things to their proper end.

Then there was Wednesday,
Wrestling my bike through Spoon Gap,
Moving like a boulder through sand
Up that brutal ascent
Partly to preserve my pride,
Partly to avoid destruction,
But mostly to reach the top,
To see things to their proper end.

And that is what you've given me,
From that very first of my days
When I interrupted a baseball game,
To the ones I pass right now,
Battling my brain like my bike,
Grinding to find some good words
To honor your living and passing,
And doggedly believing I can
Because you would believe I could,
And knowing I'd be getting help
Because you'd asked God to give me some,
And knowing I'd find that finish,
Not particularly artfully,
Nor necessarily gracefully.
Hardly ever quickly,
But unquestioningly certainly,
With a stoic tenacity,
Because I've seen you do it so many times,
Watched you see things to their proper end.

Tyler

for my stepson

I watch you, intrepid,
Nature poet reborn
Like him a bounding roe
Hearing voices of stones
Ones known but to children
I watch and follow
Where I can or I will
As you dance to some song
That plays only for you
In the wind at some peak
Or the top of some fall
And as we make our way
Over roots and rocks and trees
We become that same man.
I show you my places
And watch while you conquer
And protect when I must
And try to be Merlyn
Try to make you a king

Lights on the Half-Life

for Julie and Tyler

Captive,
The full moon peers, suspended,
its white face flecked with grey
like some tired, war sullied angel
through a cage of tree branches
my rapt attention split in three,
waiting for it to rise and escape,
watching the boy's oblivious game,
but mostly keeping nervous vigil
on the serpentine street below
and the headlights that lumber
like uncertain riders across its back,
wondering if each will be the one
that carries the other half of my heart.

Pensive,
the halting rhythm in my chest
follows this sparse flow of traffic,
keeps pace with every approach,
rising with all emerging prospects,
falling as this one takes a left,
again as that one passes us by,
then when the moon eludes the trees,
one set of lights turns to the right,
releasing me from the cold confines
of the dull half-life of her absence,
and moon, and tree, and boy, and I
am more vital since she is here,
and the whole place exudes life.

In Case Anyone Wonders

for Dewman "Buddy" Doggs

You may not agree, you may not care, but if you are holding this book you should know that of all the sights I love in this world — and there are plenty — very near the top of the list is this one: dogs without leashes.
—Mary Oliver, Dog Songs

In case anyone wonders this is joy
Mine certainly, but only by proxy
As it can only haltingly approach
The raucous runaway train that is you
Feet untrammeled to your spirit's delight
Hurtling unabashed through this minute
A wild mismash of madness and method
No posturing, pensiveness, nor pretense
Oblivious to the blustery gray
That smothers up the January sun
And as you roister like some deft Falstaff
Through this spot of time that forgets the leash
You unwittingly try to teach me things,
Of freedom, savoring moments, and love
And as I prove myself a poor pupil
You expose me for what I really am
A competent fake at all of those things
But we'll come back to school each chance we get
In hopes that I can see all this like you
Because although I may never manage
To grasp the lessons that you have for me
I never weary of watching you work.

Warmth

for Kaylen

Fearful of the cold,
I foraged through the dark playroom,
its wood floor carpeted thick with toys,
and on a shelf I found a night's salvation,
old maybe, strong yes, thick, and blue,
and that night it covered me exceeding well,
sending tendrils of real warmth to the floor,
taking care of me like one who lives there,
one who creates gifts that dwarf in all value
any that can be bought with simple dollars,
starry purple penguins around her picture,
green Leprechaun hats on St. Patrick's day,
and posters on my truck when I get home.

For hours I slept in a warm Elysium.

Crane

for Larry

I ran like hell then,
Fueled by unsullied boyish glee
And a touch of fictional fear
Until, inspired by bad design,
Turned into the path of my pursuer,
The first train I ever met,
My oldest sister's husband,
Excited seconds before the crash
Lost like so many of those days,
So many other odd memories
Escaping into the muddled haze
To forever elude my personal lore.
Addlecoved, I picked myself up
With his aid and sincere concern
And guilesssely requested another wreck.
The first of now myriad occasions
Where light proved to be locomotive
And I had to pick myself up.

You witnessed more of my collisions,
My reckless ventures into blind passages
Refusing to chastise a childhood nemesis
Or once, as a halting novice deacon
Speaking into my questioning ears
The only words which even approached
Sincerity, or wisdom, or merit of remembrance
Or together sorting out the scathing wreckage
Of the loss of your son, my nephew/brother
Or remaining to this day the only constant
The only member of my contentious family
To love me in that unassuming way
That you did that ancient summer day
When you knocked me out and picked me up
And taught me how to regroup.

Only Now

for my Dad

We were there then,
Mama, Daddy, and us, the twins,
Sprawled across that big grey porch,
Cincinnati Reds fans by proxy,
Joining the throng over AM waves,
Imbibing the background sounds of summer
And the heavy warmth of a July evening
While Mama gave me her team
And told of a dog named Bucky,
The namesake of a childhood favorite.

Daddy was with us,
Waiting for the Pirates score,
But now I wonder if that was all.

Maybe he dreamt of his home,
So close to those three rivers,
That place he had left three decades before,
Maybe as if Roberto Clemente
Could hand him a piece of PA
Through that cheap transistor box,
And place it in his hands and heart
Where he sat in that Virginia town.

It is only just now
That I shake my youthful oblivion
To think about and try to feel
With the heart of my father,
To wonder if what he left
Was worth what he came to.

The one son who left,
My late discovered brother,
The many jobs, the picket lines,
Your life some insane, incessant dance
On the floors of myriad workplaces,
Performing to provide…
Provide…provide

Only now do I realize
That was what it was.

Only now do
I ask what you kept for yourself.

Only now do I know what I missed.

Seventeen

for Julie

The first 14th reflects the seventeenth,
Like wrestling reflects most of life,
A mirror into everything or nothing,
Every happening the thing itself,
Then that layer beneath, calling,
Which so many people ignore,
Denying it like magic or truth,
But which draws me to itself like fire,
An insight that shows me that extra secret
The one that makes me what I am, gives me that edge,
That tiny broom straw in the heat of summer
That makes all the difference when I need it.

In the wake of that temporal fiasco, that fall,
What happened that night was perfect,
A moment to make William Blake proud,
A veritable marriage of heaven and hell
A definite reconciliation of opposites,
Probably the beginning of real perspective,
Another edge.

Next morning another secret came,
An epiphany as clear as that sunrise,
The only advantage I'd ever need.

I knew four things before then,
That God loved me,
That somebody would sell me books,
Somebody would sell me beer,
And that regardless of who won or lost,
I was still trying to do the same thing.
Then I realized you loved me,
And apart from God, nothing else mattered.

So today, here we are,
Drinking through a bigger disaster,
And I don't care, much,
Because what I learned back then is still true.
And that's all that matters.

Sweet Hat
(Halting Sonnet #11)

I was a giddy thing the day before
48 and a kid at Christmastime
Conflicted, and a man on that day too,
Having been warned just days prior to this
That a certain hostile congregation
of candles on my July birthday cake
will one day forge the wrong edge of the sword,

As old today as Rich was when she tried
To hold the whole of her life in one glance
An image that recurred to me all day,
Prompting me to agree that someday soon
A gaze upon the pieces of my past
I myself would be wise to undertake
But too many for a child to gather.

And that is what I was on that morning
Peeking through the freeing bars of the park
A prison I wanted to break into,
A boy genius armed with more resources
Then ever I mastered those decades past
When my dad took me out to see the team
That first made me fall in love with this one.

Forgetting both the solstice and the web
And all the things we still don't understand
Diving into the wreck of green and blue
The field and fans and grandly gothic Ds
Myself with one of each, blue shirt, green hat
A purchase that we hoped would bring us luck
And did, as our boys took both games that day

And both of us remembered other times
Revived by the place where we passed that day
Your sister and the childhood you shared there
My father and the game he gave to me
And covered in the magic of that place
Became children again for that one day
The troubles of the years left on the street

The next day marked eleven years for us
A road trip south to share a stomping ground
That I left long before we ever met
And once again the green worked out for us
The rain chasing us onto a side hike,
Not planned, but the best haunt we found that day
We wondered at treasure stumbled upon.

But you do not embody luck to me,
But providence, and grace, a second chance
To be a child if only now and then
Carried back on the crack of wooden bats
Or music from another spot of time,
To be a man whose future holds the gift
Of loving someone more than life itself.

Glances at Classrooms

Fire, Miracle, and Love

for Kade

The tale has lived for a brief decade now,
One miracle seared in my memory
Maybe infused with more power today
Because of one who saw and wrote it down
So that if the mind's images did fade
The words would raise it again from the ash
To live again and burn me with its light
But its bard makes a truly grave mistake
To believe that he was bereft of flame
Since he had fire of a different kind
Built from a scene that only happened once
Never to transpire in quite the same way
Whose luminescence might forever wane
If it had not been captured on a page
And passed around like hot and tiny sparks
To spread the glory of its principals
A story kindling now at least three fires
One for the thrower who authored the scene
A second for the bard that wrote it down
A third one for the teacher of them both
Whose conflagration blazes brighter still
Because it will be stoked eternally
With bellows spewing forth a threefold love
One held for the most excellent of sports
A second for the raw fire of the word
A third for both the thrower and the bard
And as one battle follows on the next
That moment will stand as one of the best
A song of fire, miracle and love
That demon dissolution cannot still.

Trying to Teach Rich to Seniors with Twenty-Three Days of School Left

to my Spring AP II classes, 2008

We're still Marines and we got a job to do.—Gunnery Sergeant Apone, Aliens, upon being told his troops couldn't use their rifles in an upcoming battle

Showed up at school today
with knife, camera, and book,
ready for my own little dive
to take my younglings along
when I followed Rich into the wreck.

It was NOT one of those days
in what has been an era
of perspective overkill when I have,
what seems pretty much daily,
sat stolidly in front of them and said
"This will make a great deal more sense
when you have more years behind you."

Because EVERYBODY has wrecks, right?

Mine may be bigger, darker,
more labyrinthine, more damaged,
myself a more than half damaged instrument,
but we all have ruins to explore-correct?

So I, with every ounce of the best
solitude and silence I could muster,
left them alone with the poem.
First, the colored envelopes came.

Invitations to the senior tea,
pastelled symbols of the light they sought,
and I read the names as I passed them on,
written out in full like their imminent diplomas,

Erin Marie Middlemas,
Rachel Lynne Gibson,

Harbingers of an end against whom no
poem, however wonderful, can stand.

Forlorn as the bell rang,
in an act of unwitting compassion,
Rachel Lynne, happy they got her middle name right,
showed me a drawing she made when I
used to be a superhero. Maybe.
Still, I soldiered on to third period.

And more envelopes came.

Kara Lea Ruffin,
Brian Michael Cartwright,
Katherine Joy Gilliam,

And with them the sun,
beaming through the blinds of
my darkened room, bright and warm
with its own indolent allure,
and they stopped talking to me
and I watched their lights fade,
they who had been with me for so long,
laughing at Spratling's Ode to English Class,
but still not talking to me anymore,
while Natalia Nguyen,
who has been with me for three classes,
and will make a 5 on the AP exam,
and once wrote verses to the bookman,

wrote another poem,
of the call of the courtyard outside,
a song so loud it drowned out my voice,
deciding today to agree with Whitman
that all great deeds were conceived in the open air,
and all free poems also.*

And the only things I can think of to
tell them will be tough sells,
like the light at the end of the tunnel
is more deadly than a locomotive
if it distracts us from the minute we're in,
or that wrestling,
and baseball,
and my mom all speak truth—
It matters how you finish.

Or that Madame Moore was right,
holding my face in her wizened hands
as she admonished me not to wish my life away.

But regardless of the end,
there will be no damage to me from these,
because they have learned to read and write,
not just eat and make love,
and I will stay here rejoicing in who they are,
loving them for what they bring to my wreck,
their words,
their stories,
our myths,
but no damage.

Only Treasure.

* This poem was both conceived and crafted in the open air.

Catching Muses in an Empty Room

This silence is abrupt.

It holds me here,
in a sort of dumbfounded stupor
the hands of my mind reaching,
darting into darkened corners,
trying to catch muses.

One shows me a young flame,
Filled with life and largesse,
Then wipes it away with her hand,
Until all that remains is its first spark.

Another shows me a fledgeling choir,
together a bevy of newfound voices,
then steals the sound from the landscape,
until all is reduced to one tongue.

Still another shows me teachers,
holding forth the fruits of their thought,
then makes them disappear,
until all is myself, the pensive student.

And some voice somewhere,
From that place inside me where treasure is kept,
Shouts a muffled story about the swiftness of change.

But the true muse is at my shoulder,
And she hums a tune about loss.

It makes more sense.

Fourteen

for Scott Fandetti, Todd Richardson, Scott Moffat, and the members of the '94-95 and '95-'96 Jeff County Wrestling teams

*Old men forget: yet all shall be forgot,
But he'll remember with advantages
What feats he did that day*—Shakespeare, Henry the Fifth

Fourteen.

This is an auspicious number for us.

Every August when I teach Beowulf,
I always point out that he took fourteen
Of the best and bravest, the most stalwart
Of his companions when he took to sea
And then undertook to defeat Grendel.

My students look at me as if I'm touched,
Failing to fathom my fascination
When I point out to them with overt pride
That fourteen weights make up a wrestling squad.

For nearly twice fourteen years now I have
Turned that same number over in my head,
(Of course for a while it was only twelve,
Then for an even briefer time thirteen),
Seeking the proper type of alchemy
To take fourteen and make it forty-three,
The other magic number of our kind,
The formula that converts all our time,
And toil, and sweat and lessons from defeat
And transforms them into the purest gold.

What we did then was Beowulf in reverse,
You fourteen fought while I stood by and watched
Exhorting, goading, urging, from the side,
Wanting you to be better than I was
To spread a breast much wider than my own,
As if it might confirm the width of mine,
To crush the teacher and in so doing
Reward the highest honor to my style.

And of all others you will be the first
To prove to me all that people can do
When everyone embraces an ideal
And undertakes to make reality,
And that there is one element required
To make victory sweeter even still
That without it all else is meaningless
The outward gold simply a weak veneer
Concealing something not worth possessing,
The strong love of a band of real brothers
Forged from the crucible of common toil.
Thirteen heads shaved in solidarity
Just like the boys from Taylor Mali's poem
The one declining with a witty quip,
Not with the intent to appear disloyal,
Wielding the humor that made him so fine,
And added to the love we had for him.

Because it wasn't the plaques and medals
The knowledge that we had done exactly
What it was that we had set out to do
That helped us navigate the insane grief
That fell upon us on that August day,
And beset us again twelve years later,
And then again only a month from then,
But the love that we had managed to find
Somewhere amidst the noise of all our trials,
That helped us to stand shoulder to shoulder

Against the sadness that harried us then,
And to come away with some victory,
However pyrrhic, on those forlorn fields.

And as time passes I will not forget,
(Though I might miss it by a day or two),
Your names will be, just as King Harry said,
Familiar in my mind as household words
Todd the Captain, Moffat and Fandetti,
Raley and Hodgson, Anderson, Kenner,
And a host of others to swell the ranks,
Loveday and Schrader, the younger Moffat,
McCarter, Bull and May, Evans and Brooks,
Breeden and Lindsey, McCulley are there,
As well as those before who paved the way,
Cavanah, McMahan, and Debuty,
And those who came after and played a part,
Lowe, Molzon, Garcia, Jenkins, and Cate,
And Jefferson to close the wall of fame,
These will forever in my flowing cups,
Be freshly remembered every time
I look with joy on all that's come before
Or with pause on all that may be in store,
And like Beowulf will do the proper thing,
Will thank God for all that you've given me.

Look

All things are ready if our minds be so.—Henry V

Unknown.

That's what it is really.

Step into my world,
where words burn like beacons,
and obey my every command.

That's what I want you to know,
but I will only let you look,
since you have lights of your own
that wait to answer your questions.

Paint your own starry night,
with your own fiery stones,
looted from a life of inquiries
and the answers that appear
infrequent as the gold in a stream.

Step into my world,
where words burn like beacons
and speak whatever comes to you,
and I will strive to interpret
in more than five sentences
the questions you have for me.

And lay hold of your own mind,
like a weapon of magical steel,
or a room to be furnished by you,
or a world where the answers hide
like lost children longing to be found
but will keep themselves safely hidden
until you seek them out with real desire.

Step into my world,
where words burn like beacons,
but do not be discouraged
if I answer your entreaties
with questions of my own
to force you to raise your sword
and slay your dragons
with your power

You Can't Write a Poem About Virtual Graduates

May. Battle the only thing
humming in my brain.
I walk past the deceased iron bell,
down the campus walkway,
past the aspiring adolescent rappers,
by the ROTC cadets
struggling to raise the flag
for an entirely indifferent crowd,
to my Boar's Head in Eastcheap.
they are noisy, then taciturn and torpid.
I stand in the sepulchral air.
All around me younglings are waiting-
the weight of reticence,
the pungent odor of sandalwood,
the young brains full to capacity,
drawn to the warmth beyond the windows.
When I finally give them the poem,
the entire group is struck dumb as Kimiko,
their tongues thick as baseballs,
their faces blank as the remaining pages
of their soon to be complete True Notebooks.
Suddenly I understand resignation.
As I reach for them,
they evanesce like Strahd von Zarovich,
fading and reappearing in safer climes.
I'm thinking, how remarkable it is
At this time of year, how easy
It is to be empty.
We leave together, the bell declaring them
ninety minutes closer to freedom.
I walk back past the dead old bell,
still as the ones I just left,
the flag waving at half mast
in the sultry, seductive sun,
the crowd as indifferent as ever,

wistful, my mind, spirit, and tongue
stoic with the wonder
of this ever protean world.

Pats on the Fire Line

Thanks to James Dickey

In the cool shade of our pressbox
I try to train my spirit's eyes
to infiltrate the poem shocked brains
of these twenty-nine captives.

Half musing on the backs of heads
Looking for that one whose energy
becomes the light switch in the dark
that needs to spark for us

Wishing that I could know
more fully than at this instant
if the things you have said
in the words you have left
has brightened their minds even a little
illumined by that same fire
that drew the line you saw

Because each seems to me
to be that fire line flower
thriving an inch from death
the border there drawn
by the low flame of ignorance
that creeps with consummate stealth
then sears like the flames of hell.

Thirty-Two

Antoine, don't wish your life away.—Madame Jane Moore

I have, for thirty-one whirlwind years now,
Twenty-three in this very same, safe spot,
Sat here, imbibing the calm emptiness,
Like Hamlet eating the promise crammed air
Of a classroom the day before summer
Is for all intents stolidly banished
By school's sudden, sure resurrection.

Reminded in a playful, wistful way
Of the scene in the first Rocky movie
When The Italian Stallion stood alone
In that empty, dark Philly arena,
Pondering the nature of the coming broil,
Almost certain of the contest's stark end,
Oblivious to all it would begin.

And as a metaphor it holds its own
While I muse confident, pensive, and proud,
For though I hold that same uncertainty,
I know that something sublime will ensue
Memories born from the wit of my kids
Relationships built to seal great blessings,
The treasure we'll bring to each other's lives.

But following hard on that rising joy
That comes as I anticipate the new
A stoic spirit whispers in my ear
Reminding me that while the ride's been grand
That it has carried me at breakneck speed
Forty-four years the scant distance between
Today and when I sat where they soon will.

So then the most pressing lesson appears,
That I might help them live Arthur's last hope
To learn to read and write and think and love,
Or understand Falstaff's duality,
Or how much they share with John Grady Cole,
But if I can't teach them to live right now,
I'm not sure I can lay claim to success.

So as I set my hand to one more plow,
I see the greatest task I'm bound to face
Is not to teach the fine beauty of words
But to avert their young hearts, minds and loves
From distant days that will come soon enough,
To entrench themselves in each fine moment,
To live Madame Moore's entreaty to me.

Glances at Elegy

Gifts

for Scott Fandetti

Whitman spoke of stars,
and songs, and offerings.

I thought about using his words,
but even they seem powerless
to mark this time,
this first time,
when the bagpipes played
and we traveled the circle
all clad in white,
wielding our hammers,
but without you,
and your large sweet soul we loved so well.

And we call to you now,
as we have so often since you left us
on that wicked August night,
to tell you that we come here for ourselves,
but we also come for you,
and we see you as the brightest star
to light the heavens of our memories,
and we raise our songs to you,
dirges lifted from bleeding throats and broken hearts,
the thundering peals of a score of victory cries,
and we leave our offerings for you,
the sweat of a thousand battles,
the sting from an ocean of tears,
a seat in the line where we wait,
and hammers.

But most of all,
the love of a host of brothers
and a promise to remember always.

Scars

another for Scott

Through the chilly grey
of this Tennessee winter
once again I travel,
another lost explorer
looking for the hazy gate
to my second better world
where the eyes of my soul,
so blind to so much
seek the company of your ghost.

Tiny candle beacons
burn off bits of the fog,
as I watch your image flicker,
in and out, like the right words,
and the smoky, capricious light
shows me not how you were
but how you should be now,
there in your battle dress
with all the rest of us.

It is just at that moment
that the malicious knowledge
of a now closed past
compounds the dull frustration
of a never to happen future
to create a sort of blade
that opens the old wounds anew
and allows what had once been scars
to pour out that pain once again.

Grief like this frigid breeze
Washes over my body
And I welcome it like you
And I revel in its beating,
And I know that I only hurt
Because I lost a piece of myself
To one who deserved to have it.
It tells me that I do indeed live.

I want to always remember like that.

Two Years Gone

another for Scott

Through Panels of Cloth
the spectres of strangers
escort me gently back to you,
in the junkyard of the dead.
They bring me, a friend,
and I watch with you there,
sitting with James Dickey
on the sunbaked, rusty hood
of the carcass of some Chevrolet,
talking sports, and poems,
and the girls you did them for,
waiting for Doris Holbrook
(whom I imagine is there too)
to show up one more time.

Hands

for Todd Richardson

There are lots of weak necks up here. —Chris Bull

Holding your hand there on that final night
Was the first time I realized their size
More like the great paw of some predator
Perfect tools of the task I trained them for
To take that far wrist in a brutal grip
And turn a weak neck into their embrace
And crank it till the shoulders found the mat
To stay there until victory was ours,
The same powerful hand that held a child
Suspended laughing at the thrill of height
Aloft and secure in his daddy's love.

And while my hands are not at all like yours
Our hearts beat madly with a kindred fire
Your hands joined mine when I awoke my dream
Hands helping me to set the cornerstone
Of the place I forever strive to build,
Hands driven by the same sorts of desire
By stubbornness, by anger, and by love
Like lunatics who had something to prove
To the world or to not a soul at all,
Or maybe to nobody but ourselves
Hands imposing relentless pure contempt
On any person, place, thing or idea
That found itself in the way of our dream
Or anyone so ignorant to say
That we could never reach the gold we sought,
Hands rampaging to reach the unseen heights
Sometimes with fire so indiscriminate
That we turned them on each other in rage
But never with a flame so decadent
To burn away unconditional love.

And as I toil from here to the end
It is not the hands of that final night,
Hands fighting to preserve a dying flame
That flickered, flared, and sparked until the last,
Days beyond when the ones supposed to know
Declared that it would dim to blaze no more,
That I remember as I pass my days,
But young hands from those very first of times,
Hands that held fast to an opponent's wrist
And turned the weak neck to a sure defeat
Hands stalwart, loyal, true and diligent,
Hands that bestowed on me the finest love
And faithfulness that I may ever know,
Hands whose memory will not stray from me,
Hands that I will sorely miss till the day
That my own give up their hold of this life.

A hand that held a child safe in the sky.

Where Were the Bells?

for The Hitman

We have heard the chimes at midnight, Master Shallow...Jesus, days we have seen.—Henry IV, part II

Where were the bells that day my brother?
What sort of clamor was loud enough to muffle
The heavy noise of the songs of our days,
The ones we'd seen before that instant
That you forgot, or went deaf?

How could you not remember
That Camelot is always doomed to fall
And that even if there are no grails,
Or if they are but just don't work,
We still have to try to find them,
And if we don't to figure out some way
To live with the brief shining moments,
(because they're brief, but by God, they do shine)
To learn like Wart to read and write
Instead of just eating and making love.
And your old mentor was just like Merlyn
With his weakness for feckless humanity.
Instead you locked him in a cage,
His only company the forlorn realization
That he again tried to make kings of men and failed.

Didn't you believe the memories we made
Were better than mansions or dwelling places?
I thought they were fortresses impregnable,
Like The Hornburg too tough to be breached
Defended by at least one tenacious dwarf
And a crew of the most unlikely allies
But looks like I was wrong another time
To you it must have been Tortilla Flat

Where, taking a cue from our pal Danny
You took the cliff into the afterlife
As we, the musing comrades, watched you go
While in the background, fiery and final,
The houses we shared gave in to the flames
Which endured in their marvelous insanity
Until only a desert remained there.

So in this flood eternal I travail
On the small island that used to be yours
Bailing madly with a punctured bucket
In a round puddle that won't see the sun
Until the day I get to where you are
Until then I will always be puzzled
At how long you were rained out of the light
And how one of my favorite young seeds
Could forget and drown without a good brawl
And I'll hear your voice when the tall ships go
And sometimes even lose a little sleep
And hold you in my keep of remembrance
And miss you every mile that I run
But never once will I see it your way.

Glances Outside

Sanctuary

Initially,
I hesitate.

As is the case with so much
that requires an exercise of will
I ponder the nature of challenge,
and wonder if the effort is relevant.

But the water beckons.

So tentatively,
I enter this late summer stream,
pausing periodically
as my body adjusts to the shock of the cold,
asking myself if this is the limit,
allowing an insane sort of patience to drive me,
up to my neck, into this imitation of winter,
realizing that I have wandered onto a kind of field
where inner fire and outer frost battle.

At first, the stream seems to perceive my presence
as some act of aggression, myself the interoper,
and directs the whole of its force to my repulsion.

And with this we understand each other,
because if this is a fight, I am in my element,
sensing something to win, something to oppose,
oblivious to the fact that the waters never yield,
merely permitting its own momentary capitulations,
secure in the fact that it will abide
long after I return to my world,
but for now tolerating this alien visitor,
perhaps at the behest of its higher power,
since certainly I feel Him there.

He permeates this place,
silent as the stones who stand sentinel here,
but larger, so large, like some Titan,
a Guard ever vigilant, poised between all
from which I seek momentary respite.

But He does not speak,
And the silence is quizzical.

Not begrudging the still, small voice,
refusing to equate silence with absence,
but at this time craving a shout
that will shake the trees in this place
and rearrange the constellations
arrayed in this wildly lucid night sky.

Still, nothing presents itself,
save the persistent presence,
and the immutable mystery,
and the sweet sensations
of this momentary peace.

And that is enough.

Dreary Intercourse

for she can so inform
The mind that is within us, so impress
With quietness and beauty, and so feed
With lofty thoughts, that neither evil tongues,
Rash judgments, nor the sneers of selfish men,
Nor greetings where no kindness is, nor all
The dreary intercourse of daily life,
Shall e'er prevail against us, or disturb
Our cheerful faith, that all which we behold
Is full of blessings.—William Wordsworth

Where are you now, nature poet,
And what were the particulars of existence
That midst the din of towns and cities
Brought on the hours of weariness
That led you to seek your sweet sensations?

Today is Wednesday, on this day I rose
A bit early so I would have the time
To set my day within a proper frame
But all my good intentions were for naught
That fifteen extra minutes lost somehow
Attending to the monarchs of my life
Indifferent to the beauty of the stones
Which call to me from these rocky pastures
That lie throughout the valley where I live
Coupled well with the deep blue of the sky
That chose to grace this one late winter morn.

I turned my eye from nature in my haste
And plunged once more into the sticky webs
That tangle up my life from day to day
Vainly sounding out to some fine future
For moments when I just might find repose
And take time to look at the life of things.

All that I seem to see right now are hands
Each grasping for a small piece of my time
These obligations I cannot escape
And which surround me more from day to day
It seems that, reaching for experience,
I've taken on legions more than I should
And cannot find scant seconds to reflect
On all I have so fiercely fought to gain.

And midst the rush of all that lunacy
A bolt of clarity strikes me head on,
That if I cannot find a little peace
My gospel will be empty and inept
To those I wish so greatly to convert
That if my heart is powerless to feel
The joy derived from finding just one poem
And seeing through it I am not alone
Then how can I convince those in my charge
That all the searching is indeed worthwhile?

How can I manage to communicate
That this is something we should add to life
When I myself am busied by so much
That separates me from the very things
I tell them they so desperately need?

Then through this clamor Wordsworth sounds a chord
Reminding me of how in lonely rooms
He drew upon the past to find a cure
For all the poisons coursing through his brain
And so his pupil I resolved to be
To engage in a little exercise
To find a way to teleport myself
To some place where I would perhaps find strength.

At first I tried to retreat to last fall,
Sitting on a stone high in the Smokies,
Above the peaks of many smaller points
Above the clouds that swallowed up the day,
Above the mists licking foothills like waves
Of some mystical pool that makes its way
To our world for a time then takes its leave
Half expecting some grand leviathan
To rise forlornly from this mystic place
And stamp its presence on the hills and trees
Before the rising sun forced its retreat
Along with the white loch that was its home,
A place forever captured in my mind,
In a way that transcends the images
That we create with all our fine machines
Because it is one that is wholly mine
Preserved precisely as I perceived it
Still, it taught me the lesson that sometimes
Sunshine is not the day's finest decking.

Ode to The Smokies
(the unwitting conclusion to Dreary Intercourse)

I call her healer, church, and remedy

Perhaps it is an entry of a sort,
an advance to primeval or pristine,
a return to some better beginning,
some sweet recapture of so much once lost
a search for some essential innocence
where we can all be unspotted again
if only for the briefest spots of time.

I used to jump from aircraft,
so many seconds of pretentious flight,
one swallow, a scant mouthful of this peace
the wind singing an esoteric song
one reserved only for the blessed souls
who get to ride those flimsy nylon wings
mimicking the action of the eagle.

And every time those feathers fell to earth,
returning my body to solid ground,
I'd lie face up in the grass like a child
checking hurriedly each inch of my frame
and, once assured that all was unbroken,
would swagger off to find all my playmates,
high on adrenaline and full of tales.
I check my soul that way when I am here,
Trusting the cold water of mountain streams
And the cleansing soil of much traveled paths
To purge from me the tenacious poisons
That threaten to cut off my life each day
I pay forced homage to reality.

And even though we've brought our rat race here
ignorant of our interloping ways,
rolling on in slow moving metal tents
packing with us our disrespect of space,
I still manage to find a dose of life,
some safe house from which to plan my next move,
some buffer between me and all the dark.

I like to think that one day I'll just walk,
saying goodbye to all that makes me weak
and pitch my tent and never ever leave
this haven filled with pure peace and muses
and know the joy that Elric must have felt
when he discovered fabled Tanelorn
that keep that shielded him from all sorrow.

Dwell with my healer, church, and remedy,

Little Bighorn

No trumpets or war cries now
Nought but the midsummer breeze
Perhaps the tortured songs
Of the souls who roam this place
Yearning to tell true tales
Of all that passed that day
Debunking the myriad myths
Surrounding just how they fell
Seeking a single strong voice
A solitary mourner to hear the dirge
Managing but frustrated whispers
In a language unintelligible
Except to rise as an anthem
To the now ironic tranquility
Of the chaos that once raged there

Beartooth Pass

It was one of those things I came to find.

Myself, alone,
standing in that mountain meadow,
the landscape like some palette
that God had used at one time
and then just left there,
small samples of His best work,
smatches of stark and stony grey,
rolling, soft, friendly green pastures
dotted with royal purple flowers,
His voice whispering in the breeze,
and snowdrifts in mid-July,
and trees.

And then there was me.

But I was no alien here,
rather a witness to this power,
and I found a stand of trees,
a horseshoe, like some shrine
where some sage, solitary priest
might make contact with heaven,
but no holy man was there then,
so I became him for a time,
and got to sense the strength
coursing through that copse,
and I knew what Wordsworth meant
when he spoke of that presence
that disturbed him with the joy
of elevated thoughts. I felt that
And I didn't want to leave
Because I sensed beyond doubt
That I was in a holy place,
That nothing could harm me,
That for that spot of time,
I was as large as anything there.

Andrews Bald (based on Dover Beach by Matthew Arnold)

for Julie on Valentine's Day 2009

The sky is clear today,
The grass so green, the sun shines here
Upon the bald; below, Fontana Lake winds,
Serpentine and sure, and is gone, lost
Like a wanderer in the woods and hills.
Sit with me here, and see what I have found!

Here, on the bare side of the hill,
Where thick forest surrenders to the Heath,
Look! I watch the verdant space
Bereft of trees, pausing in their advance,
To see with us, in this high spot,
The power of a place of primal peace,
Its silence puissant and rampant too,
Singing its song of gladness and rebirth.

Wordsworth long ago
Saw it on the Wye, and it brought
Into his mind the sense sublime,
Of elevated thoughts; we
Find also in the sight a joy,
Witness it in this cloistered patch of spring.

My mount of loss
Was once, too, when this same place
I visited alone in the misty fog,
But now only I see
It leveled by the strength of your presence,
Crumbling, to the knowledge
Of you here in this place, stones and pebbles,
And rubble, created by you here.

Ah, love, we will be true
To one another! And this world,
Which some say is no land of dreams at all,
So insane, so absurd, so fleeced,
Will have some joy, some love and light,
Security, solace, and peace for us,
And we stand in this place of life and might
Half hoping that we'd never have to leave
While those misled resume their futile fight.

In Praise of Rain (September 21, 1998)

The thunder came this morning
Its distant voice vaguely familiar
like a loved but seldom seen friend
One welcome but out of place
So I stopped where I stood,
Perplexed, waiting to confirm
That these Zeusian rumblings
Were actually overhead,
That I was actually awake,
That this arid juggernaut
Which had run so long amok
And then raised its siege,
Leaving all so scorched and sere,
Had finally found a challenger,
If only for today.

Then lightning launched its brightness
Dim against this grey morning sky,
But there as well, though distant,
Like the last recollection
Of a morning like this one
When the rain kissed my windshield
And chased the fainthearted inside,
And I embraced these two companions,
These long awaited harbingers of fall,
I called them my liberators
From monotony, and humidity,
And the dust that blanketed all,
And the dry ground now ready

To accept the sign in my yard
To take seed as a symbol of rebirth

Milligan Station on The Tweetsie Trail

I sought for a subject, that should give equal room and freedom for description, incident, and impassioned reflections on men, nature, and society, yet supply in itself a natural connection to the parts, and unity to the whole.—Samuel Taylor Coleridge

It doesn't exactly fit
My definition of going to the woods.

First,
There is too much visible civilization,
Too many roads in ready view
Like sneaky devils whispering
pestiferously in my anguished ear
that no matter what nature says
unabashed progress is still king,
Too many cars in easy earshot
like boorish but tenacious bards
singing a pitchy, persistent anthem
In praise of untrammeled prosperity,
Too plainly pristine the gravelly trail,
like putting clean clothes on Pigpen,
A competent but self-evident impostor,
Just a short step from a city sidewalk.

Second,
There are too many bicycles,
Most of them innocuous enough
But a certain faction in sufficient number,
Indulging their raw racing fantasies,
Punishing their pedals like van Aert,
In view of yet another podium,
Oblivious to others on the trail,
tearing through space like madmen in a rage,
almost as if a wolfish Van der Poel
was clinging like a fiend to their back tires

wringing their handlebars, hellbent for speed,
Forsaking every point of etiquette
Each admonition posted on the way,
Tranquility the last thing on their minds

But…
If a person finds themselves a far piece
From any serious stretch of wilderness
Then climbing to the quarry might just do
If you turn your back to the busy trail
And focus on the waters far below
Or if you sit down on the other side
And get your eyes to just the right angle,
Avoiding glances at the school below
And between the pervasive power lines
It is possible to catch a decent glimpse
Of one of Wordsworth's sweet pastoral farms
Green to the very door just as he wrote
Surrounded by his sportive woods run wild
And find a smatch of nature to be yours.

Glances at Forms

The Sleep

How do we fight the sleep that we abhor?
And muster up the might at close of day
To sweep the cobwebs from the dusty door

While some contend that there is nothing more
And sit content with not a word to say
How do we fight the sleep that we abhor?

With dull frustration I observe this war
And wonder where to search to find a way
To sweep the cobwebs from the dusty door

The riddle rings as loudly as before
The question comes in tones of near dismay
How do we fight the sleep that we abhor?

Could we join battle with a raging roar
And like some stalwart knight resolve to stay
To sweep the cobwebs from the dusty door?

Could we resolve to then craft our own lore?
To contribute our own verses to the play?
To fiercely fight the sleep that we abhor
And sweep the cobwebs from the dusty door

Prine

It is the blight man was born for/It is Margaret you mourn for—Gerard Manley Hopkins, *Spring and Fall*

Like you I hate graveyards and old pawnshops
Singing like sirens dirges of loves lost
Scraping to salve an ache that never stops
Caring, full heedless of my heartbreak's cost
And like you I long endlessly to ride
That great green river where paradise lay
Blind to the truth impossible to hide
That time's stern toll has taken it away
And like the girl who grieved for Goldengrove
I gaze outside myself when I see death
The concept still abstract, feckless to move
Me while I walk this world and still draw breath
Yet I am not so simple not to see
The man for whom I really grieve is me.

The Table

Like Shadows of a fate too fell to fight
The blood of Uther thundered through his veins
Growing up in a world beset by might
He'd witnessed his own father's brutal reign
Merlyn, having seen history, knew well
Depredations had held stark sway so long
Knew that to prevent this quick coming hell
That reason must redress the realm's old wrongs
So the young monarch went wisely to work
Tasked by his mentor to propose a plan
Rooting out lairs where base lawlessness lurked
That might's madness need never rule again
And when Merlyn spoke Zachariah's prayer
He knew his pupil might the realm repair

The Grail

Gawaine was first to be sent bootless back
Irascible, his anger like a stain
Disdain for Galahad made plain his lack
The glory of the cup he would not gain
The Paisanos quested to save their king
Possessed of free time like a priceless jewel
Their toil that day a legendary thing
But Danny refused healing like a fool
And me, more than once in this life have found
My little kingdoms compromised by threat
And while I fight to hold my sacred ground
Flawless Camelot I have not kept yet
But still King Arthur's idea blazes bright
Like that last house in the Monterrey night

Three Crowns, Three Hundred, Three Thousand

Batting third, and playing first base-The Big Man, Miguel Cabrera—Jim Price

Since sixty-seven Yaz stood all alone
Claiming his three crowns and making his mark
You were so adored when you won your own
You got a standing O in Royals Park
I had the luck to be there in the crowd
The day you launched three hundred from the yard
The crack of that moonshot lovely and loud
To you it seemed like anything but hard
And on this day, a perfect one for ball
You shot one through the hole on the right side
Another step toward Cooperstown Hall
Myself ecstatic to have watched your ride
I thank the baseball gods to be so blest
To witness wonders from one of the best

de la Rocha's Keys-A Sestina

If you hate something, don't you do it too.—Eddie Vedder

Why don't you just admit it's about money?
And if it's not give me the deeds and keys
To that high dollar Ford and house-see the reactions
That will fill the pages of mags and books
When you lend integrity to your music
Instead of throwing some hypocritical party

And since you have such disdain for parties
Why not take some of that capitalist money
That you make off your raging music
And give some poor oppressed folks a key
To your house or Explorer or buy some books
For all the unenlightened and watch their reactions

And while we're on the topic of reactions
I have to chuckle at your recent party
Your pals who think they've read the same books
And who are making all that same money
Do they possess the same array of keys
That you've racked up trading on your music?

The things you decry in all your music
Brings out in me some quite mixed reactions
Drowned out by the rattle of all your keys
As you toss them in pocket and party
Since some wealthy folk don't have your money
Or high capitalist grades in their books

Will the future remember you in books
As one who made a difference with your music
Or simply a capitalist who made money
By combining words to elicit reactions
Pretending to oppose this or that party
While those same systems gave you all your keys?

One Steady Glance

I can't block out the rattle of your keys
Since I've read in a great many good books
That the very same systems and parties
Against which you rail in all your music
Seem to share with you the same reactions
As the ones you've picked up with your money

Sorry that your keys are louder than your music
Let the books note here that my reaction
Is that it's all a party to make you money

Glances at Random

Jesus of Mitchell
(Christ at The Corn Palace)

I saw You that day,
Three foot figure behind the fence,
scarred palms extended to us
like some stoic third base coach
signaling his runner to stop,
or a teacher pleading for peace,
or one question at a time,
while one short block away
The multitudes converged, enthralled,
on a palace made of corn,
and we shared a laugh
at the absurdity of it all,
and as I sit now I know
that You could hit a curve,
but it slipped my mind to ask
if You had dug Wall Drug.

The Heaven of Hillbillies

Apologies to James Dickey

Here I sit. The red light burning.
If they are looking for food,
It is Food Lion.
If needing airbrushed magick,
It is a shirt shack,
A small piece of Pigeon Forge.

Having new checks, they have come,
Anyway, to this their heaven.
The green light lets them in.

And they come.
The wide eyes open.

They mock them, the real florists,
Copying, desperately
Copying what they have done:
A cheaper rose,
A plastic vase.

For some of these,
It could not be the place
It is, without deals.
These hunt, as they have done
But with all stores under one roof.

More bargains than they can believe
They shop more eagerly
And rifle through racks of clothes
And their purchase
Of tons of bargain merchandise
May take days
In an endless array of lines

And those that are waiting
Know this as their life,
Their reward: to shop

Under such shelves in full knowledge
Of all the sales that await them
And to feel no fear
But ecstatic elation
Fulfillment with dollars to spare.

At the point of ingress
I am stuck, I sit
Under the light
I come, I get stuck,
I go, get stuck again.

Rhode Island Plate
(or the tale of Sir Daniel and Sir Jeffrey-for J.D. Lambert)

We undertook your quest,
that day a pair of surrogate champions,
and we found your holy grail
in a parking lot in South Dakota.

In that same place,
we passed your next five tests,
and completed all your labors
before three suns had set.

The we pointed our steeds west
And like a pair of knights errant
Rode off to conquer Hell's Gate
And feel the breath of God.

We only wished you rode with us.

Hymn to Halloween

I raise my hearty hymn to Halloween
and its fell legion of the setting sun,
the fearful faces that haunt us at night,
in their various forms of monster
be they vampire, or zombie,
werewolf or white-masked slasher,
bearing grins rictal or malevolent,
and the colors that they wear,
midnight's black, pallor's grey,
the ever essential red,
and the shadowy climes that they inhabit,
where Freddy Kreuger's always funny mean,
and Michael Myers never seems to run.

I lift my song of thanks
to the icons of the evening,
from the star-crossed Strahd,
to the living dead,
the hellraising Pinhead,
or The Knight of the Black Rose,
held safely in prisons of celluloid,
perhaps bound in leather or loose leaf,
but free to walk our mental landscapes,
regaling them with darkness all the way,
securing their eternal hiding place,
where Freddy Kreuger's always funny mean,
and Michael Myers never seems to run.

I craft a fearful tune,
for the homes of the grotesque,
from Cthulu's Miskatonic U,
to the mists of Ravenloft,
the odd avenues of Bangor, Maine,
or the ruins of Myth Drannor,
locales that mete their harrowing torments
on the lost souls who pass dour days in them,
not caring to discriminate at all,
the horrors that they hand out equally,
where Freddy Kreuger's always funny mean,
and Michael Myers never seems to run.

My verse turns to respect
for those who stand as champions of light,
from old Van Helsing or Van Richten,
to the bold Fellowship of Middle Earth,
the unwitting Bill Denbrough and his crew,
or Vorhees' myriad antagonists,
all those who willingly or otherwise
squared off with this collection of grotesques,
and showed us where the silver bullets are,
or becoming God's madmen in that place
where Freddy Kreuger's always funny mean,
and Michael Myers never seems to run.

I find my voice of praise
For the builders of these macabre worlds,
From Hawthorne to Poe,
To King and Barker,
Stoker and Shelly,
Lovecraft, and recently strong Cam Collins,
The ones who have opened our eyes
To alluring pictures of fright
That seem to attract us somehow,
Whenever we gaze on those distant lands,
where Freddy Kreuger's always funny mean,
and Michael Myers never seems to run.

At last I speak a melancholy dirge
for the ones who miss the trip
from clerics and teachers
to those who take all so seriously
the ones who out of fear or ignorance
or whoever they might be
and think that fantasy is wrong
fearing satan or some other Bugbear
and never seem to see that there are times
we need to take our leave from this real world
on a trip to some other dark country
where Freddy Kreuger's always funny mean,
and Michael Myers never seems to run.

Glances Inside

Pendragon and Perez

The fate of this man or that man was less than a drop, although it was a sparkling one, in the great blue motion of the sunlit sea.—T.H. White

Listening to Arthur,
standing at the end of something,
thinking of what is mine,
my own brief shining moments,
my own small sparkling drops,
but the ocean seems not at all vast,
on the contrary, it looms largely small,
like all the yards in this place
grade school gridirons and diamonds,
so sufficiently spacious swift decades past,
now scant, merely patches of turf,
and my senses shift, sounding elsewhere
for the ghost of my father
and a night when, on this same porch,
with a different radio, the Big Red Machine
traded a Tony Perez RBI single
for a win on the way to a pennant (I think).
And the scene replays itself,
But then fades and brings me back.

Now I am the Tyger, Thomas the Lamb,
Now things are once more small,
And time is the smallest of all,
Now I yearn for my own clutch hit,
And I long to sit with Arthur,
And wish for my own ocean,
Looking for my own drops,
Searching for my own sparkles,
Which at present escape my sight.

Song of Myself #13

This is me,
the crafty rogue
who steals all the gold I can carry
Then runs for eternity without spending a cent.

Never looking back,
Never realizing that no one is chasing me.

Not for the Lovers

Pining for pipesmoke and Paradise's milk,
Celtic tunes in random array,
Sharpwriters and loose leaf
and a sparsely lit night,
longing to create that place,
with all its trappings,
where I make my own fragile magic.

Not for the lovers, who cannot help me now,
their land more fictitious than Tanelorn.
The joy of love a rapid fading shade,
the pain of love bereft a musing best ignored,
refusing the false solace of trite self-pity,
puzzling over the necessity, importance
of churning out these self-indulgent scripts.

And the answer comes to me.

For my demons. For a fight.

Time Stand Still

Belly down,
bathed in sweat,
I grasp time by the wrists
as it hangs from this cliff
like an unfortunate companion
but try I as might
He slips stoically from my hold
and plummets silently down
to join his broken brethren
on the floor of that canyon
strewn with the skeletal husks
and the well mangled wrecks
of frivolity and good intention

Emrys

That day he threw fire

That one rainy day,
He taught himself the runes,
Burned them into his brain
And when the time came
For him to work his art
Remembered them.

He felt the blaze
As the flames leapt forth
From his heart to his lips
To the tips of his fingers
Standing bathed in the glow
Long after the flame was spent.

When it was finished,
He walked off alone.

That day he was Merlyn,
And nobody knew it but him.

No Matter

I

It seemed no harder then,
Three ascending miles of asphalt
In plodding cadence towards the top
Legs burning but strong enough
Lungs pounding but with air enough
Forty pounds and thirteen years
The heavy space between today
And the first time I got on a bike
With the still Odyssian intent
Of trekking myriad miles and miles
And, resolve unblunted by time's escape
Completed the task I set for myself.
It seemed no slower then, but it was.

II

It seemed much simpler then,
Blank sides filled with words,
An exhalation of halting breaths,
A spewing forth of feeble fire,
But feeling an oblivious sort of strength
Because the runes worked for me
However tenuous they may have been
Scores of sharp pencils and five years
The tangled space between today
And the last time I took out a page
With the possibly Quixotic notion
That my words might just bring flame,
To be like Arthur and rally the clans
Of the tales that run free in my brain.
It shouldn't be harder, but it is.

III

But I ponder the first lesson,
Holding up now next to then
And I see yet one more thing to learn.
I may have lost traces of speed and grace
While gaining lethargy and girth
But when the peaks are all reached
And the chain grabs the big ring,
When blank pages are finally full,
And an army of words assembled,
The feeling is the same now as then,
That same puissant, unique rush
That filled me on the first day.
Then easy or hard is no matter.

Chainsong

Too many hands on my time.—Neil Peart

Like berserker hordes,
words rage across my brain
smashing walls and lighting fires,
their frenzied battle tempered
by their faith in a captain
who will arise one day
to organize them smartly
into perfect ranks and files
and guide them on their way
as they invade blank pages
in perfect formations,
so sadly unaware
that their chieftain lies weak
chained to a wall of reality
held behind bars of taken time
waiting for them to set him free.

Musing

I think the occasional safe battle is healthy
This short study of tension and surrender,
And I wonder if actual war is like this,
Some fight, some lie down, and just why,
This day conscripts on a voluntary patrol,
Some sitting with weapons in hand,
Others fallen by their own protection,
So I decide to force a few to take arms.
Some grudgingly shoulder the musket,
And I wonder what will happen to them
When their battles decide a world more
Than a grizzled commander's praise.
Will they fight, or just fall down, and why,
And exactly what their losses will be,
This short study of tension and surrender,
This death to the sleep of more than body.

To Prufrock

In time past

I thought I would not go with you
Reluctant to take a tearful jaunt
Through your personal Nadsokor,
Crawling over your twisting ruins
Smoky with the wrecks of futile purpose
Thick with the entropy of paralyzed force
The seedy hotels,
The tawdry restaurants,
The disprized loves,
And lost days.

I had my own versions of those,
A Motel Six on the edge of Fort Benning,
The smell of my own stale beer,
The despair of a legion of rejections,
And close to fifty forever fugitive years,
And I like mine better than yours,
Because I find life in the destruction,
And blessings in the rot,
And love other side of the rubble.

Last March all my moments flickered
While the Footman held my coat and laughed
As he led two of my people away,
And I was not scared, but stolid,
Not terrified, just tuckered,
A whoreson round man going down
Like a ragged assed renegade
Under an assault of sack and sugar.

Then I decided to fight again.

And now I think maybe
That really was not it at all,
Not what you meant at all,
And that we are more alike than I think,
That we would shave our heads
And point
And laugh
At the stuffed ones kissing broken stone
And the mawkish Danish princes,
At all the merciless login
And the brutally absurd momentum
Of the juggernaut of time and experience.

And die all, die merrily.

Hidden, Found

Hidden, found,
Secrets sing
shining white
like tempests,
like whispers,
lost to eyes,
lost to flesh
hidden truths
hard torments
lost to us.

Hidden, found,
Angels fly,
shining grey
like urchins,
like soldiers,
lost to crowds,
lost to time
hidden suns
hard visions
lost to us

Hidden, found,
Poems die,
shining not
like secrets,
like angels,
lost to you
lost to me
hidden joys
hard secrets,
lost to us.

Lessons from a Storm

for Melanie Glenn

Later that night, the boat was in the middle of the lake, and he was alone on land. He saw the disciples straining at the oars, because the wind was against them. Shortly before dawn he went out to them, walking on the lake...Immediately he spoke to them and said, "Take courage! It is I. Don't be afraid." Then he climbed into the boat with them, and the wind died down.—Mark 6:47-51

My morning broke quietly with this tale,
And halting to divine one day's wisdom,
Some knowledge that I possibly might live,
It impressed me for maybe the first time,
How, peering through a boy's much darker glass,
Perhaps there was a finer point I missed,
In this story, told to me since childhood,
More as a statement on Christ's wondrous might,
The obstacles He deftly casts aside
With a skill that defies all similes,
No metaphor to match his massive strength,
Might hold a different message for a man.
But first I had to realize myself,
That a man was exactly who He was,
Like me part human, like me part divine,
A mere man, twenty summers my junior,
Could, with confidence complete and supreme,
Born of both an adamantine faith
And love that baffles all we understand,
Walk upon a malign and windy lake
To reach the disciples placed in His charge
And still the tempest that beleaguered them
Not so much as a show of puissance
As a display of deep and perfect love.

It was then that my musings turned to you,
As you attempt to navigate this time,
Your winds of pain, perplexity, and loss,
Keeping you from the light that you deserve,
At that point I must shamefully confess
That while my faith will never be enough
That I might walk the surface of a lake,
It will place me inside that boat with you,
Pulling at the oars with all the strength I have,
Faith enough to believe He will find us,
And with love enough to be here for you
We'll find some shore of wisdom and of sense.

What I Can and Can't

I want to hunt like David
I want to kill me a giant man
I want to slay my demons
But I've got lots of them, I've got lots of them
—Noah Gundersen, David

There are only three names I'd like to have,
A holy trinity of life well lived
But won't presume to claim them for myself
Since plainly that pretension seems to me
An act of more than overweening pride
So all that I can do is my labor
Hoping that in the courses of my life
Those whose paths have mingled with my own
Will find the grace to grant them all to me

One name I covet madly is Maestro
Like Merlyn, Jacob Kahn, or the Blackstaff,
Beginning with a vision of great things
For those who come under my tuition
To always receive the best of my gifts
Then blending persistence, passion and pride
Just like the alloys of a perfect sword
Forged as a weapon for the aid of man
I'd make my charge's world a better place

Another name I'd wish to have is Real
Like Mal Reynolds, Han Solo, or Samwise
Emptied of craft, duplicity, or guile
Seen as a person of integrity
With all my faults tattooed upon my sleeve
So even if I rankle now and then
Or fail to fit into the proper peg
At least I can say I am who I am
And hope that doesn't cause anyone pain

But more than those I want the name Loving
Like Kolbe, Saint Francis, or Jonathan
To manifest that greatest gift of all
More powerful than prophecy or words
More abiding even than faith or hope
More radiant than knowledge or wisdom
A love so luminescent and so loud
That it trumped my foibles, failures, and faults
But that name may be one past wishing for

Still, I can claim duality defined
White's Gawaine, Falstaff, Peter my patrons
The first a slave to anger's two edged sword
The second subject only to his heart
The third a wild mishmash of faith and doubt
Loving God but ignoring His wisdom
Intimately aware that mostly I'm
A bastard but God loves me anyway
Following in the footsteps of those three

Acknowledgements

W.H. Auden said that poets weren't lonely, but that poetry was in the sense that nobody reads it.

First, I want to thank Julie, because she's read most of the poems I've ever written, since most of the ones I've written over the past twenty-four years have been for her, ranging from silly Valentine's sonnets to serious treatments of the difference she makes in my life. Thank you. I love you more than anything.

I want to thank my stepson Tyler Berrier and his partner, Francesco Deiana, for the thoughtful cover art. When I started thinking about doing this I knew I wanted them to design my cover.

I want to thank the folks I'm pretty sure read at least some of these poems (see the Auden quote)-Russell Minatel, Kiki Garman-Diamond, Will Koella, Matt Sanders, Jamie White, Julianna Maeng, and Kade Jenkins. I also want to thank Kade for writing my foreword and pushing me to undertake this project.

I'm going to thank my friend and favorite brewmaster, Marty Velas, for the beer he promises to create in my honor after this is actually published. He is more than a man and less than a god when it comes to making beer, so I know it will be excellent.

Thanks to Alex Kinder for helping me with the formatting.

I want to thank Dr. R.R. Turner for introducing me to Walt Whitman, my gateway into poetry, and to Kay Senter for tasking me with teaching poetry when I served as her student teacher back in 1991. That was where I met the English Romantics and W.H. Auden, who drew me completely into the genre.

I want to thank Walt Whitman for making poetry both accessible and something I thought I could write, W.H. Auden for drawing me in with his humor and benign self-deprecation, James Dickey for showing me what he called "the poet as a man of action," Mary Oliver for perhaps being the most aware human being I have ever read, and Adrienne Rich for *Toward the Solstice* and showing me the interplay between literal and figurative. I hope to visit you all in the afterlife.

Finally, I want to thank every student and athlete I've had the privilege and honor of attempting to mentor. You have brought treasure to my wreck and are one of the joys of my life.

About the Author

Jeff Price is now in his thirty-second year as an English teacher, twenty-three at Science Hill High School in Johnson City, Tennessee. He also taught at Abingdon High School in Abingdon, Virginia, and Jefferson County High School in Dandridge, Tennessee. He just completed thirty-eight years coaching wrestling on the high school, college, and middle school levels. His career earned him a spot in the Tennessee Chapter of the National Wrestling Hall of Fame and has included stops at Waggener High School in Louisville, Kentucky, Carson-Newman College in Jefferson City, Tennessee, Abingdon High School, Jefferson County High School, Science Hill High School, and finally Liberty Bell Middle School in Johnson City. He currently resides in Johnson City with his wife Julie, as well as a trio of cats—Merlyn, Mister, and Cleo, and his boon companion, Dewman "Buddy" Doggs, the rescue dog who rescued him.

www.ingramcontent.com/pod-product-compliance
Lightning Source LLC
Chambersburg PA
CBHW020944090426
42736CB00010B/1250